Presented to:

Luke Redden

On the occasion of:

Christmas 2002

By:

Candace Leamon

Date:

Dec 25 /2002

Other books in the God's Promises series:
GOD'S PROMISES FOR MOTHERS

North American edition published 2000 Augsburg Fortress, Publishers, Minneapolis.

Original edition published in Denmark
under the title *God's Promises for Fathers* by Scandinavia Publishing House,
Drejervej 11-21, DK-2400 Copenhagen NV, Denmark.
Tel. (45) 35 310330. Fax (45) 35310334. E-mail: jvo@scanpublishing.dk

Quotations and paintings selected by Scandinavia Publishing House
Edited by Tomas Vium Olesen
Design by Ben Alex
Cover painting by Viggo Pedersen, 1888 (Statens Museum for Kunst)
Printed in India
ISBN 0-8066-4098-7

GOD'S PROMISES

FOR FATHERS

Augsburg
MINNEAPOLIS

God's Promises for Fathers is more than a nice-looking gift book, a delight to the eye. Meditate on the verses in the silence of your heart. Allow the beauty of the art to uphold the wisdom of the words.

It is a privilege to spend time with our heavenly Father, and it is the hope of those who put this book together that it will provide guidance in your daily walk with God. When Jesus walked the earth, He had a very close relationship with God, calling Him His Father. We too can walk closely with God. No longer does Jesus call us servants; instead He calls us friends, because everything He learned from His Father He has made known to us. We are His brothers and God is our Father.

All we have to do is stay close to God. How can we do that? One way is to read His Word. There we receive the encouragement and strength we need. He will help us succeed as good fathers, teaching us in the ways of love, mercy, and patience—all characteristics of His own personality.

OTTO HASLUND

My son, keep my words
and store up my commands within you.
Keep my commands and you will live;
guard my teachings as the apple of your eye.

Proverbs 7:1-2

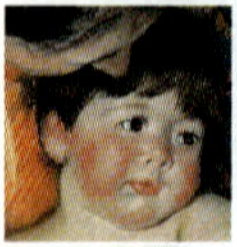

Love

See, I have engraved you on the palms of my hands;
your walls are ever before me.

Isaiah 49:16

Better a meal of vegetables where there is love
than a fattened calf with hatred.

Proverbs 15:17

Keep yourselves in God's love as you wait for the mercy
of our Lord Jesus Christ to bring you to eternal life.

Jude 21

May your unfailing love be my comfort,
according to your promise to your servant.

Psalm 119:76

Constantin Hansen

As the Father has loved me, so have I loved you. Now remain in my love. If you obey my commands, you will remain in my love, just as I have obeyed my Father's commands and remain in his love. I have told you this so that my joy may be in you and that your joy may be complete. My command is this: Love each other as I have loved you. Greater love has no one than this, that he lay down his life for his friends. You are my friends if you do what I command. I no longer call you servants, because a servant does not know his master's business. Instead, I have called you friends, for everything that I learned from my Father I have made known to you. You did not choose me, but I chose you and appointed you to go and bear fruit—fruit that will last. Then the Father will give you whatever you ask in my name.

This is my command: Love each other.

JOHN 15:9-17

Guidance

He will not let your foot slip—
he who watches over you will not slumber;
indeed, he who watches over Israel
will neither slumber nor sleep.
The Lord watches over you—
the Lord is your shade at your right hand;
the sun will not harm you by day,
nor the moon by night.

PSALM 121:3-6

As you sent me into the world, I have sent them into the world. For them I sanctify myself, that they too may be truly sanctified.

JOHN 17:18-19

Walter Leistikow

His eyes are on the ways of men; he sees their every step.

JOB 34:21

Where can I go from your Spirit?
Where can I flee from your presence?
If I go up to the heavens, you are there;
if I make my bed in the depths, you are there.
If I rise on the wings of the dawn,
if I settle on the far side of the sea,
even there your hand will guide me,
your right hand will hold me fast.
If I say, "Surely the darkness will hide me
and the light become night around me,"
even the darkness will not be dark to you;
the night will shine like the day,
for darkness is as light to you.

PSALM 139:7-12

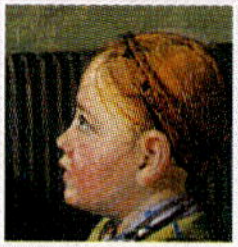

Upbringing

My son, do not despise the Lord's discipline
and do not resent his rebuke,
because the Lord disciplines those he loves,
as a father the son he delights in.

PROVERBS 3:11-12

Discipline your son, for in that there is hope;
do not be a willing party to his death.
A hot-tempered man must pay the penalty;
if you rescue him, you will have to do it again.
Listen to advice and accept instruction,
and in the end you will be wise.

PROVERBS 19:18-20

MARIA BASHKIRTSEFF

For you know that we dealt with each of you as a father deals with his own children, encouraging, comforting and urging you to live lives worthy of God, who calls you into his kingdom and glory.

1 THESSALONIANS 2:11-12

Preach the Word; be prepared in season and out of season;
correct, rebuke and encourage—with great patience
and careful instruction.

2 TIMOTHY 4:2

The rod of correction imparts wisdom,
but a child left to himself disgraces his mother.
When the wicked thrive, so does sin,
but the righteous will see their downfall.
Discipline your son, and he will give you peace;
he will bring delight to your soul.

PROVERBS 29:15-17

Fathers, do not exasperate your children; instead,
bring them up in the training and instruction of the Lord.

EPHESIANS 6:4

Responsibility

And do not forget to do good and to share with others,
for with such sacrifices God is pleased.

HEBREWS 13:16

The righteous care about justice for the poor,
but the wicked have no such concern.

PROVERBS 29:7

Who then is the faithful and wise manager, whom the master puts in charge of his servants to give them their food allowance at the proper time? It will be good for that servant whom the master finds doing so when he returns. I tell you the truth, he will put him in charge of all his possessions.

LUKE 12:42-44

Whoever can be trusted with very little
can also be trusted with much, and whoever is dishonest
with very little will also be dishonest with much.

LUKE 16:10

The tongue has the power of life and death,
and those who love it will eat its fruit.

PROVERBS 18:21

Anyone, then, who knows the good he ought to do
and doesn't do it, sins.

JAMES 4:17

VENIĆIAN

Direction

I am the light of the world.
Whoever follows me will never walk in darkness,
but will have the light of life.

John 8:12

Stern discipline awaits him who leaves the path;
he who hates correction will die.

Proverbs 15:10

I am the Lord your God,
who teaches you what is best for you,
who directs you in the way you should go.

Isaiah 48:17

ILJA REPIN

For these commands are a lamp,
this teaching is a light,
and the corrections of discipline
are the way to life.

PROVERBS 6:23

I will instruct you and teach you in the way you should go;
I will counsel you and watch over you.

PSALM 32:8

A man's steps are directed by the Lord.
How then can anyone understand his own way?

PROVERBS 20:24

Wisdom

Be warned, my son, of anything in addition to them.
Of making many books there is no end,
and much study wearies the body.
Now all has been heard; here is the conclusion of the matter:
Fear God and keep his commandments,
for this is the whole duty of man.

ECCLESIASTES 12:12-13

Four things on earth are small, yet they are extremely wise:
Ants are creatures of little strength,
yet they store up their food in the summer;
conies are creatures of little power,
yet they make their home in the crags;
locusts have no king, yet they advance together in ranks;
a lizard can be caught with the hand, yet it is found in kings' palaces.

PROVERBS 30:24-28

THEO VAN RYSSELBERGHE

Who is wise and understanding among you?
Let him show it by his good life, by deeds done
in the humility that comes from wisdom. But if you harbor
bitter envy and selfish ambition in your hearts, do not boast about it
or deny the truth. Such "wisdom" does not come down from heaven
but is earthly, unspiritual, of the devil. For where you have envy
and selfish ambition, there you find disorder and every evil practice.
But the wisdom that comes from heaven is first of all pure;
then peace-loving, considerate, submissive, full of mercy and
good fruit, impartial and sincere. Peacemakers who sow in peace
raise a harvest of righteousness.

JAMES 3:13-18

Listen to advice and accept instruction,
and in the end you will be wise.

PROVERBS 19:20

Work

Watch out! Be on your guard against all kinds of greed;
a man's life does not consist in the abundance of his possessions.

LUKE 12:15

The Lord will open the heavens, the storehouse of his bounty,
to send rain on your land in season and to bless
all the work of your hands.

DEUTERONOMY 28:12

Whatever you do, work at it with all your heart,
as working for the Lord, not for men, since you know that
you will receive an inheritance from the Lord as a reward.
It is the Lord Christ you are serving.

COLOSSIANS 3:23-24

All hard work brings a profit,
but mere talk leads only to poverty.

PROVERBS 14:23

In vain you rise early
and stay up late,
toiling for food to eat—
for he grants sleep to those he loves.

PSALM 127:2

Do not work for food that spoils,
but for food that endures to eternal life,
which the Son of Man will give you.
On him God the Father has placed
his seal of approval.

JOHN 6:27

Ministry

A farmer went out to sow his seed. As he was scattering the seed, some fell along the path; it was trampled on, and the birds of the air ate it up. Some fell on rock, and when it came up, the plants withered because they had no moisture. Other seed fell among thorns, which grew up with it and choked the plants. Still other seed fell on good soil. It came up and yielded a crop, a hundred times more than was sown.

LUKE 8:5-8

I planted the seed, Apollos watered it, but God made it grow. So neither he who plants nor he who waters is anything, but only God, who makes things grow. The man who plants and the man who waters have one purpose, and each will be rewarded according to his own labor. For we are God's fellow-workers; you are God's field, God's building.

1 CORINTHIANS 3:6-9

VINCENT VAN GOGH

Your attitude should be the same as that of Christ Jesus:
Who, being in very nature God,
did not consider equality with God something to be grasped,
but made himself nothing,
taking the very nature of a servant,
being made in human likeness.

PHILIPPIANS 2:5-7

And we urge you, brothers, warn those who are idle,
encourage the timid, help the weak, be patient with everyone.

1 THESSALONIANS 5:14

He who is kind to the poor lends to the Lord,
and he will reward him for what he has done.

PROVERBS 19:17

Leadership

Plans fail for lack of counsel,
but with many advisers they succeed.

PROVERBS 15:22

Be shepherds of God's flock that is under your care, serving as overseers—not because you must, but because you are willing, as God wants you to be; not greedy for money, but eager to serve; not lording it over those entrusted to you, but being examples to the flock. And when the Chief Shepherd appears, you will receive the crown of glory that will never fade away.

1 PETER 5:2-4

The Lord does not look at the things man looks at.
Man looks at the outward appearance,
but the Lord looks at the heart.

1 SAMUEL 16:7

Francois Gerard

The tongue has the power of life and death,
and those who love it will eat its fruit.

PROVERBS 18:21

You know that the rulers of the Gentiles lord it over them, and their high officials exercise authority over them. Not so with you. Instead, whoever wants to become great among you must be your servant, and whoever wants to be first must be your slave— just as the Son of Man did not come to be served, but to serve, and to give his life as a ransom for many.

MATTHEW 20:25-28

He must manage his own family well and see
that his children obey him with proper respect.

1 TIMOTHY 3:4

Vision

When your days are over and you rest with your fathers, I will raise up your offspring to succeed you, who will come from your own body, and I will establish his kingdom. He is the one who will build a house for my Name, and I will establish the throne of his kingdom for ever. I will be his father, and he shall be my son. When he does wrong, I will punish him with the rod of men, with floggings inflicted by men. But my love will never be taken away from him, as I took it away from Saul, whom I removed from before you. Your house and your kingdom shall endure for ever before me; your throne shall be established for ever.

2 SAMUEL 7:12-16

Where there is no revelation, the people cast off restraint; but blessed is he who keeps the law.

PROVERBS 29:18

For God does speak—now one way, now another—
though man may not perceive it. In a dream, in a vision of the night,
when deep sleep falls on men as they slumber in their beds,
he may speak in their ears and terrify them with warnings,
to turn man from wrongdoing and keep him from pride,
to preserve his soul from the pit, his life from perishing by the sword.

JOB 33:14-18

I swear by myself, declares the Lord,
that because you have done this and have not
withheld your son, your only son, I will surely bless you
and make your descendants as numerous as the stars in the sky
and as the sand on the seashore. Your descendants will take
possession of the cities of their enemies, and through
your offspring all nations on earth will be blessed,
because you have obeyed me.

GENESIS 22:16-18

Priorities

No one can serve two masters. Either he will hate the one and love the other, or he will be devoted to the one and despise the other. You cannot serve both God and Money.

MATTHEW 6:24

Blessed are they whose ways are blameless,
who walk according to the law of the Lord.
Blessed are they who keep his statutes
and seek him with all their heart.
They do nothing wrong; they walk in his ways.
You have laid down precepts that are to be fully obeyed.
Oh, that my ways were steadfast
in obeying your decrees!
Then I would not be put to shame
when I consider all your commands.

PSALM 119:1-6

PAUL GAUGUIN

My dear brothers, take note of this: Everyone should be quick to listen, slow to speak and slow to become angry, for man's anger does not bring about the righteous life that God desires.

JAMES 1:19-20

Be very careful, then, how you live—not as unwise but as wise, making the most of every opportunity, because the days are evil. Therefore do not be foolish, but understand what the Lord's will is.

EPHESIANS 5:15-17

If anyone would come after me, he must deny himself and take up his cross and follow me. For whoever wants to save his life will lose it, but whoever loses his life for me will find it. What good will it be for a man if he gains the whole world, yet forfeits his soul? Or what can a man give in exchange for his soul?

MATTHEW 16:24-26

Marriage

It is not good for the man to be alone.
I will make a helper suitable for him.

GENESIS 2:18

Drink water from your own cistern,
running water from your own well.
Should your springs overflow in the streets,
your streams of water in the public squares?
Let them be yours alone, never to be shared with strangers.
May your fountain be blessed,
and may you rejoice in the wife of your youth.

PROVERBS 5:15-18

Auguste Renoir

For this reason a man will leave his father and mother and be united to his wife, and the two will become one flesh.

EPHESIANS 5:31

You have stolen my heart, my sister, my bride;
you have stolen my heart
with one glance of your eyes,
with one jewel of your necklace.
How delightful is your love, my sister, my bride!
How much more pleasing is your love than wine,
and the fragrance of your perfume than any spice!
Your lips drop sweetness as the honeycomb, my bride;
milk and honey are under your tongue.
The fragrance of your garments is like that of Lebanon.

SONG OF SONGS 4:9-11

What God has joined together, let man not separate.

MATTHEW 19:6

Wife

How beautiful you are, my darling!
Oh, how beautiful!
Your eyes behind your veil are doves.
Your hair is like a flock of goats
descending from Mount Gilead.
Your teeth are like a flock of sheep just shorn,
coming up from the washing.
Each has its twin; not one of them is alone.
Your lips are like a scarlet ribbon; your mouth is lovely.
Your temples behind your veil are like the halves of a pomegranate.
Your neck is like the tower of David, built with elegance;
on it hang a thousand shields, all of them shields of warriors.
Your two breasts are like two fawns,
like twin fawns of a gazelle
that browse among the lilies.

SONG OF SONGS 4:1-5

Christian Dalsgaard

Husbands, love your wives, just as Christ loved the church and gave himself up for her to make her holy, cleansing her by the washing with water through the word, and to present her to himself as a radiant church, without stain or wrinkle or any other blemish, but holy and blameless. In this same way, husbands ought to love their wives as their own bodies. He who loves his wife loves himself.

EPHESIANS 5:25-28

He who finds a wife finds what is good
and receives favor from the Lord.

PROVERBS 18:22

A wife of noble character who can find?
She is worth far more than rubies.
Her husband has full confidence in her
and lacks nothing of value.
She brings him good, not harm, all the days of her life.

PROVERBS 31:10-12

Generations

I write to you, dear children,
because your sins have been forgiven on account of his name.
I write to you, fathers, because you have known him who is
from the beginning. I write to you, young men,
because you have overcome the evil one.
I write to you, dear children, because you have known the Father.
I write to you, fathers, because you
have known him who is from the beginning.
I write to you, young men, because you are strong,
and the word of God lives in you,
and you have overcome the evil one.

1 John 2:12-14

The glory of young men is their strength,
gray hair the splendor of the old.

Proverbs 20:29

Remember the days of old;
consider the generations long past.
Ask your father and he will tell you,
your elders, and they will explain to you.

DEUTERONOMY 32:7

But my righteousness will last for ever,
my salvation through all generations.

ISAIAH 51:8

We will not hide them from their children;
we will tell the next generation
the praiseworthy deeds of the Lord,
his power, and the wonders he has done.

PSALM 78:4

Franz Bohumil Doubek

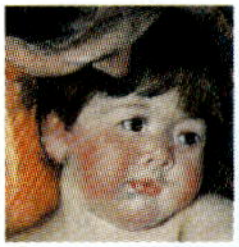

Infancy

What is man that you are mindful of him,
the son of man that you care for him?
You made him a little lower than the angels;
you crowned him with glory and honor
and put everything under his feet.

HEBREWS 2:6-7

I was appointed from eternity,
from the beginning, before the world began.

PROVERBS 8:23

Your hands made me and formed me;
give me understanding to learn your commands.

PSALM 119:73

MARY CASSATT

Let us make man in our image, in our likeness, and let them rule over the fish of the sea and the birds of the air, over the livestock, over all the earth, and over all the creatures that move along the ground.

GENESIS 1:26

Otto Haslund

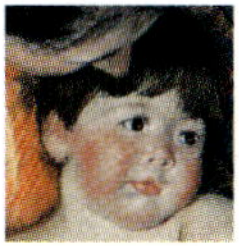

Childhood

The righteous man leads a blameless life;
blessed are his children after him.

PROVERBS 20:7

Let the little children come to me, and do not hinder them,
for the kingdom of God belongs to such as these. I tell you the truth,
anyone who will not receive the kingdom of God like
a little child will never enter it.
And he took the children in his arms,
put his hands on them and blessed them.

MARK 10:14-16

Discipline your son, and he will give you peace;
he will bring delight to your soul.

PROVERBS 29:17

Children, obey your parents in the Lord, for this is right.
"Honor your father and mother"—which is the first commandment
with a promise— "that it may go well with you and that
you may enjoy long life on the earth."

EPHESIANS 6:1-3

All your sons will be taught by the Lord,
and great will be your children's peace.

ISAIAH 54:13

Train a child in the way he should go,
and when he is old he will not turn from it.

PROVERBS 22:6

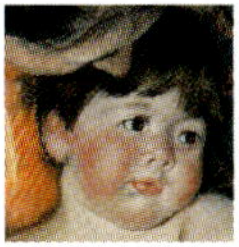

Adolescence

My son, keep your father's commands
and do not forsake your mother's teaching.
Bind them upon your heart for ever; fasten them around your neck.
When you walk, they will guide you;
when you sleep, they will watch over you;
when you awake, they will speak to you.
For these commands are a lamp, this teaching is a light,
and the corrections of discipline are the way to life,
keeping you from the immoral woman,
from the smooth tongue of the wayward wife.

PROVERBS 6:20-24

And we urge you, brothers, warn those who are idle, encourage the timid, help the weak, be patient with everyone.

1 THESSALONIANS 5:14

Similarly, encourage the young men to be self-controlled.
In everything set them an example by doing what is good.
In your teaching show integrity, seriousness and soundness of speech that cannot be condemned, so that those who oppose you may be ashamed because they have nothing bad to say about us.

TITUS 2:6-8

He who rebukes a man will in the end gain more favor
than he who has a flattering tongue.

PROVERBS 28:23

Fathers, do not embitter your children,
or they will become discouraged.

COLOSSIANS 3:21

PETER HANSEN

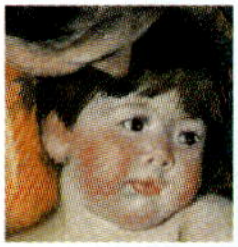

Young Adult

For this reason a man will leave his father and mother and be united to his wife, and they will become one flesh.

GENESIS 2:24

These, then, are the things you should teach. Encourage and rebuke with all authority. Do not let anyone despise you.

TITUS 2:15

Be happy, young man, while you are young,
and let your heart give you joy in the days of your youth.
Follow the ways of your heart and whatever your eyes see,
but know that for all these things
God will bring you to judgment.

ECCLESIASTES 11:9

PEDER SEVERIN KRØYER

A wise son brings joy to his father,
but a foolish son grief to his mother.

PROVERBS 10:1

Be strong and courageous, because you will lead these people to inherit the land I swore to their forefathers to give them. Be strong and very courageous. Be careful to obey all the law my servant Moses gave you; do not turn from it to the right or to the left, that you may be successful wherever you go. Do not let this Book of the Law depart from your mouth; meditate on it day and night, so that you may be careful to do everything written in it. Then you will be prosperous and successful. Have I not commanded you? Be strong and courageous. Do not be terrified; do not be discouraged, for the Lord your God will be with you wherever you go.

JOSHUA 1:6-9

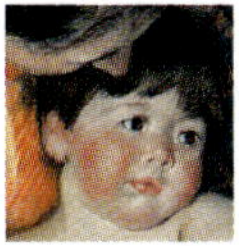

Grandchildren

Know therefore that the Lord your God is God; he is the faithful God, keeping his covenant of love to a thousand generations of those who love him and keep his commands.

DEUTERONOMY 7:9

A good man leaves an inheritance for his children's children, but a sinner's wealth is stored up for the righteous.

PROVERBS 13:22

When Israel saw the sons of Joseph, he asked, "Who are these?" "They are the sons God has given me here," Joseph said to his father. Then Israel said, "Bring them to me so that I may bless them." Now Israel's eyes were failing because of old age, and he could hardly see. So Joseph brought his sons close to him, and his father kissed them and embraced them.

GENESIS 48:8-10

Then we your people, the sheep of your pasture,
will praise you for ever;
from generation to generation
we will recount your praise.

PSALM 79:13

But from everlasting to everlasting
the Lord's love is with those who fear him,
and his righteousness with their children's children.

PSALM 103:17

They will live in the land I gave to my servant Jacob,
the land where your fathers lived. They and their children and
their children's children will live there for ever, and
David my servant will be their prince for ever.

EZEKIEL 37:25

ERNST JOSEPHSON

Wrestling

No weapon forged against you will prevail,
and you will refute every tongue that accuses you.
This is the heritage of the servants of the Lord,
and this is their vindication from me.

ISAIAH 54:17

So Jacob was left alone, and a man wrestled with him till daybreak. When the man saw that he could not overpower him, he touched the socket of Jacob's hip so that his hip was wrenched as he wrestled with the man. Then the man said, "Let me go, for it is daybreak."
But Jacob replied, "I will not let you go unless you bless me."
The man asked him, "What is your name?"
"Jacob," he answered.
Then the man said, "Your name will no longer be Jacob, but Israel,
because you have struggled with God and
with men and have overcome."

Caspar Wolf

Jacob said, "Please tell me your name."
But he replied, "Why do you ask my name?"
Then he blessed him there.

Genesis 32:24-29

Finally, be strong in the Lord and in his mighty power.
Put on the full armor of God, so that when
the day of evil comes, you may be able to stand your ground,
and after you have done everything, to stand. Stand firm then,
with the belt of truth buckled round your waist, with the breastplate
of righteousness in place, and with your feet fitted with the readiness
that comes from the gospel of peace. In addition to all this, take up
the shield of faith, with which you can extinguish all the flaming
arrows of the evil one. Take the helmet of salvation and the sword of
the Spirit, which is the word of God. And pray in the Spirit on
all occasions with all kinds of prayers and requests. With this
in mind, be alert and always keep on praying for all the saints.

EPHESIANS 6:10-18

The prayer of a righteous man is powerful and effective.

JAMES 5:16

Anxiety

How long, O Lord? Will you forget me for ever?
How long will you hide your face from me?
How long must I wrestle with my thoughts
and every day have sorrow in my heart?
How long will my enemy triumph over me?

PSALM 13:1-2

Therefore I tell you, do not worry about your life, what you will eat or drink; or about your body, what you will wear. Is not life more important than food, and the body more important than clothes?

MATTHEW 6:25

Do not be anxious about anything, but in everything, by prayer and petition, with thanksgiving, present your requests to God.

PHILIPPIANS 4:6

Trials

Though you have made me see troubles, many and bitter, you will restore my life again; from the depths of the earth you will again bring me up. You will increase my honor and comfort me once again.

PSALM 71:20-21

Blessed is the man who perseveres under trial, because when he has stood the test, he will receive the crown of life that God has promised to those who love him.

JAMES 1:12

My prayer is not that you take them out of the world but that you protect them from the evil one.

JOHN 17:15

LOVIS CORINTH

It is better to take refuge in the Lord than to trust in man.

PSALM 118:8

Awake, O Lord! Why do you sleep?
Rouse yourself! Do not reject us for ever.
Why do you hide your face
and forget our misery and oppression?
We are brought down to the dust;
our bodies cling to the ground.
Rise up and help us;
redeem us because of your unfailing love.

PSALM 44:23-26

Do not be afraid of those who kill the body but cannot kill the soul. Rather, be afraid of the One who can destroy both soul and body in hell. Are not two sparrows sold for a penny? Yet not one of them will fall to the ground apart from the will of your Father. And even the very hairs of your head are all numbered. So don't be afraid; you are worth more than many sparrows.

MATTHEW 10:28-31

Brokenness

God opposes the proud but gives grace to the humble.
Humble yourselves, therefore, under God's mighty hand,
that he may lift you up in due time.

1 PETER 5:5-6

For whoever exalts himself will be humbled,
and whoever humbles himself will be exalted.

MATTHEW 23:12

The righteous cry out, and the Lord hears them;
he delivers them from all their troubles.
The Lord is close to the broken-hearted
and saves those who are crushed in spirit.

PSALM 34:17-18

ALBERT EDELFELT

If only my anguish could be weighed
and all my misery be placed on the scales!
It would surely outweigh the sand of the seas–
no wonder my words have been impetuous.
The arrows of the Almighty are in me,
my spirit drinks in their poison;
God's terrors are marshaled against me.

JOB 6:2-4

The Spirit of the Lord is on me,
because he has anointed me
to preach good news to the poor.
He has sent me to proclaim freedom for the prisoners
and recovery of sight for the blind,
to release the oppressed.

LUKE 4:18

Perseverance

In a certain town there was a judge who neither feared God nor cared about men. And there was a widow in that town who kept coming to him with the plea, "Grant me justice against my adversary." For some time he refused. But finally he said to himself, "Even though I don't fear God or care about men, yet because this widow keeps bothering me, I will see that she gets justice, so that she won't eventually wear me out with her coming!" And the Lord said, "Listen to what the unjust judge says. And will not God bring about justice for his chosen ones, who cry out to him day and night? Will he keep putting them off? I tell you, he will see that they get justice, and quickly."

LUKE 18:2-8

Let us not become weary in doing good, for at the proper time we will reap a harvest if we do not give up.

GALATIANS 6:9

Therefore, since we are surrounded by such a great cloud of witnesses, let us throw off everything that hinders and the sin that so easily entangles, and let us run with perseverance the race marked out for us.

HEBREWS 12:1

As you know, we consider blessed those who have persevered. You have heard of Job's perseverance and have seen what the Lord finally brought about. The Lord is full of compassion and mercy.

JAMES 5:11

Do you not know that in a race all the runners run, but only one gets the prize? Run in such a way as to get the prize. Everyone who competes in the games goes into strict training. They do it to get a crown that will not last; but we do it to get a crown that will last for ever. Therefore I do not run like a man running aimlessly; I do not fight like a man beating the air.

1 CORINTHIANS 9:24-26

Illness

Like a shepherd's tent my house
has been pulled down and taken from me.
Like a weaver I have rolled up my life,
and he has cut me off from the loom;
day and night you made an end of me.
I waited patiently till dawn, but like a lion he broke all my bones;
day and night you made an end of me.
I cried like a swift or thrush, I moaned like a mourning dove.
My eyes grew weak as I looked to the heavens.
I am troubled; O Lord, come to my aid!"
But what can I say?
He has spoken to me, and he himself has done this.
I will walk humbly all my years because of this anguish of my soul.
Lord, by such things men live; and my spirit finds life in them too.
You restored me to health and let me live.

ISAIAH 38:12-16

FREDERIC BAZILLE

Nevertheless, I will bring health and healing to it; I will heal my people and will let them enjoy abundant peace and security.

Jeremiah 33:6

My days are swifter than a runner;
they fly away without a glimpse of joy.
They skim past like boats of papyrus,
like eagles swooping down on their prey.
If I say, 'I will forget my complaint,
I will change my expression, and smile,'
I still dread all my sufferings,
for I know you will not hold me innocent.
Since I am already found guilty,
why should I struggle in vain?

Job 9:25-29

Grief and Mourning

For sighing comes to me instead of food;
my groans pour out like water.
What I feared has come upon me;
what I dreaded has happened to me.
I have no peace, no quietness;
I have no rest, but only turmoil.

JOB 3:24-26

By the rivers of Babylon we sat and wept
when we remembered Zion. . . .
How can we sing the songs of the Lord
while in a foreign land?

PSALM 137:1, 4

But I cry to you for help, O Lord;
in the morning my prayer comes before you.
Why, O Lord, do you reject me and hide your face from me?
From my youth I have been afflicted and close to death;
I have suffered your terrors and am in despair.
Your wrath has swept over me; your terrors have destroyed me.
All day long they surround me like a flood;
they have completely engulfed me.
You have taken my companions and loved ones from me;
the darkness is my closest friend.

PSALM 88:13-18

I am the resurrection and the life.
He who believes in me will live, even though he dies;
and whoever lives and believes in me will never die.

JOHN 11:25-26

FRANTS HENNINGSEN

Healing

Surely he took up our infirmities and carried our sorrows,
yet we considered him stricken by God,
smitten by him, and afflicted.
But he was pierced for our transgressions,
he was crushed for our iniquities;
the punishment that brought us peace was upon him,
and by his wounds we are healed.

ISAIAH 53:4-5

When she heard about Jesus, she came up behind him in the crowd and touched his cloak, because she thought, "If I just touch his clothes, I will be healed." Immediately her bleeding stopped and she felt in her body that she was freed from her suffering.

MARK 5:27-29

Gustav Klimt

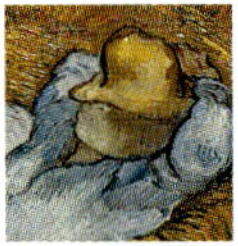

Recovery

Come to me, all you who are weary and burdened, and I will give you rest. Take my yoke upon you and learn from me, for I am gentle and humble in heart, and you will find rest for your souls. For my yoke is easy and my burden is light.

MATTHEW 11:28-30

Do you not know? Have you not heard?
The Lord is the everlasting God, the Creator of the ends of the earth.
He will not grow tired or weary,
and his understanding no one can fathom.
He gives strength to the weary and increases the power of the weak.
Even youths grow tired and weary, and young men stumble and fall;
but those who hope in the Lord will renew their strength.
They will soar on wings like eagles; they will run and not grow weary,
they will walk and not be faint.

ISAIAH 40:28-31

VINCENT VAN GOGH

Stand at the crossroads and look;
ask for the ancient paths,
ask where the good way is, and walk in it,
and you will find rest for your souls.

JEREMIAH 6:16

Praise the Lord, O my soul;
all my inmost being, praise his holy name.
Praise the Lord, O my soul,
and forget not all his benefits–
who forgives all your sins
and heals all your diseases,
who redeems your life from the pit
and crowns you with love and compassion,
who satisfies your desires with good things
so that your youth is renewed like the eagle's.

PSALM 103:1-5

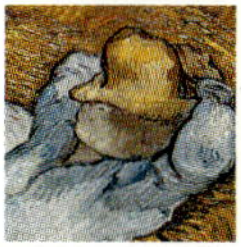

Reconciliation

Jacob looked up and there was Esau, coming with his four hundred men; so he divided the children among Leah, Rachel and the two maidservants. He put the maidservants and their children in front, Leah and her children next, and Rachel and Joseph in the rear. He himself went on ahead and bowed down to the ground seven times as he approached his brother. But Esau ran to meet Jacob and embraced him; he threw his arms around his neck and kissed him. And they wept.

GENESIS 33:1-4

Pleasant words are a honeycomb,
sweet to the soul and healing to the bones.

PROVERBS 16:24

Vilhelm Hammershøi

All this is from God, who reconciled us to himself through Christ and gave us the ministry of reconciliation: that God was reconciling the world to himself in Christ, not counting men's sins against them. And he has committed to us the message of reconciliation.

2 Corinthians 5:18-19

For if, when we were God's enemies, we were reconciled to him through the death of his Son, how much more, having been reconciled, shall we be saved through his life!

Romans 5:10

When he had received the drink, Jesus said, "It is finished." With that, he bowed his head and gave up his spirit.

John 19:30

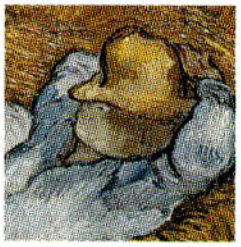

Blessing

Blessed is the man who does not walk
in the counsel of the wicked
or stand in the way of sinners or sit in the seat of mockers.
But his delight is in the law of the Lord,
and on his law he meditates day and night.
He is like a tree planted by streams of water,
which yields its fruit in season and whose leaf does not wither.
Whatever he does prospers.

PSALM 1:1-3

Blessed is he whose transgressions are forgiven,
whose sins are covered. Blessed is the man
whose sin the Lord does not count against him
and in whose spirit is no deceit.

PSALM 32:1-2

CHRISTIAN KROGH

Blessed are you who are poor,
for yours is the kingdom of God.
Blessed are you who hunger now,
for you will be satisfied.
Blessed are you who weep now,
for you will laugh.
Blessed are you when men hate you,
when they exclude you and insult you
and reject your name as evil,
because of the Son of Man.
Rejoice in that day and leap for joy, because great is your reward in heaven. For that is how their fathers treated the prophets.

LUKE 6:20-23

You give me your shield of victory,
and your right hand sustains me;
you stoop down to make me great.

PSALM 18:35

Happiness

Rejoice with those who rejoice;
mourn with those who mourn.

ROMANS 12:15

Finally, my brothers, rejoice in the Lord!
It is no trouble for me to write the same things to
you again, and it is a safeguard for you.

PHILIPPIANS 3:1

Rejoice in the Lord and be glad, you righteous;
sing, all you who are upright in heart!

PSALM 32:11

CAMILLE PISSARRO

A cheerful look brings joy to the heart,
and good news gives health to the bones.

PROVERBS 15:30

Blessed are all who fear the Lord,
who walk in his ways.
You will eat the fruit of your labor;
blessings and prosperity will be yours.
Your wife will be like a fruitful vine
within your house;
your sons will be like olive shoots
round your table.
Thus is the man blessed
who fears the Lord.

PSALM 128:1-4

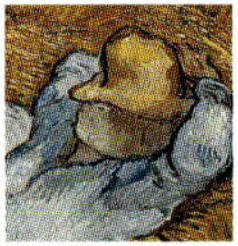

Success

One man gives freely, yet gains even more;
another withholds unduly, but comes to poverty.
A generous man will prosper;
he who refreshes others will himself be refreshed.

PROVERBS 11:24-25

With man this is impossible,
but with God all things are possible.

MATTHEW 19:26

That is why, for Christ's sake, I delight in weaknesses,
in insults, in hardships, in persecutions, in difficulties.
For when I am weak, then I am strong.

2 CORINTHIANS 12:10

May the Lord answer you when you are in distress;
may the name of the God of Jacob protect you.
May he send you help from the sanctuary and
grant you support from Zion.
May he remember all your sacrifices
and accept your burnt offerings.
May he give you the desire of your heart
and make all your plans succeed.
We will shout for joy when you are victorious
and will lift up our banners in the name of our God.
May the Lord grant you all your requests.
Now I know that the Lord saves his anointed;
he answers him from his holy heaven
with the saving power of his right hand.
Some trust in chariots and some in horses,
but we will trust in the name of the Lord our God.

PSALM 20:1-7

Conversion

For as high as the heavens are above the earth,
so great is his love for those who fear him;
as far as the east is from the west,
so far has he removed our transgressions from us.

PSALM 103:11-12

Therefore confess your sins to each other
and pray for each other so that you may be healed.

JAMES 5:16

Search me, O God, and know my heart;
test me and know my anxious thoughts.
See if there is any offensive way in me,
and lead me in the way everlasting.

PSALM 139:23-24

Jean Francois Millet

The time has come, he said.
The kingdom of God is near. Repent and believe the good news!

MARK 1:15

This is the message we have heard from him and declare to you: God is light; in him there is no darkness at all. If we claim to have fellowship with him yet walk in the darkness, we lie and do not live by the truth. But if we walk in the light, as he is in the light, we have fellowship with one another, and the blood of Jesus, his Son, purifies us from all sin. If we claim to be without sin, we deceive ourselves and the truth is not in us. If we confess our sins, he is faithful and just and will forgive us our sins and purify us from all unrighteousness. If we claim we have not sinned, we make him out to be a liar and his word has no place in our lives.

1 JOHN 1:5-10

Growth of the Spirit

Therefore, brothers, since we have confidence to enter the Most Holy Place by the blood of Jesus, by a new and living way opened for us through the curtain, that is, his body, and since we have a great priest over the house of God, let us draw near to God with a sincere heart in full assurance of faith, having our hearts sprinkled to cleanse us from a guilty conscience and having our bodies washed with pure water. Let us hold unswervingly to the hope we profess, for he who promised is faithful. And let us consider how we may spur one another on towards love and good deeds. Let us not give up meeting together, as some are in the habit of doing, but let us encourage one another—and all the more as you see the Day approaching.

HEBREWS 10:19-25

HUGO SIMBERG

A good tree cannot bear bad fruit,
and a bad tree cannot bear good fruit.

MATTHEW 7:18

Those who belong to Christ Jesus have
crucified the sinful nature with its passions and desires.
Since we live by the Spirit, let us keep
in step with the Spirit.

GALATIANS 5:24-25

Let the wise listen and add to their learning,
and let the discerning get guidance—
for understanding proverbs and parables,
the sayings and riddles of the wise.

PROVERBS 1:5-6

Prayer

He who has ears, let him hear.

MATTHEW 11:15

Glory in his holy name;
let the hearts of those who seek the Lord rejoice.
Look to the Lord and his strength; seek his face always.

PSALM 105:3-4

With this in mind, we constantly pray for you, that our God may count you worthy of his calling, and that by his power he may fulfill every good purpose of yours and every act prompted by your faith. We pray this so that the name of our Lord Jesus may be glorified in you, and you in him, according to the grace of our God and the Lord Jesus Christ.

2 THESSALONIANS 1:11-12

Dear friends, if our hearts do not condemn us,
we have confidence before God and receive from him anything
we ask, because we obey his commands
and do what pleases him.

1 John 3:21-22

And when you stand praying,
if you hold anything against anyone,
forgive him, so that your Father in heaven
may forgive you your sins.

Mark 11:25

Again, I tell you that if two of you on earth
agree about anything you ask for, it will be done
for you by my Father in heaven.

Matthew 18:19

Worship

Praise the Lord. Praise the Lord from the heavens,
praise him in the heights above.
Praise him, all his angels, praise him, all his heavenly hosts.
Praise him, sun and moon, praise him, all you shining stars.
Praise him, you highest heavens and you waters above the skies.
Let them praise the name of the Lord,
for he commanded and they were created.
He set them in place for ever and ever;
he gave a decree that will never pass away.

PSALM 148:1-6

Praise be to the God of Shadrach, Meshach and Abednego, who has sent his angel and rescued his servants! They trusted in him and defied the king's command and were willing to give up their lives rather than serve or worship any god except their own God.

DANIEL 3:28

HALFDAN EGEDIUS

Believe me, woman, a time is coming when you will worship the Father neither on this mountain nor in Jerusalem. You Samaritans worship what you do not know; we worship what we do know, for salvation is from the Jews. Yet a time is coming and has now come when the true worshipers will worship the Father in spirit and truth, for they are the kind of worshipers the Father seeks. God is spirit, and his worshipers must worship in spirit and in truth.

JOHN 4:21-24

Great and marvelous are your deeds, Lord God Almighty.
Just and true are your ways, King of the ages.
Who will not fear you, O Lord,
and bring glory to your name?
For you alone are holy.
All nations will come
and worship before you,
for your righteous acts have been revealed.

REVELATION 15:3-4

Scripture Meditation

In the beginning was the Word, and the Word was with God,
and the Word was God.

JOHN 1:1

Man does not live on bread alone,
but on every word that comes from the mouth of God.

MATTHEW 4:4

As the rain and the snow come down from heaven,
and do not return to it without watering the earth
and making it bud and flourish,
so that it yields seed for the sower and bread for the eater,
so is my word that goes out from my mouth:
It will not return to me empty, but will accomplish what I desire
and achieve the purpose for which I sent it.

ISAIAH 55:10-11

Blessed is the one who reads the words of this prophecy, and blessed are those who hear it and take to heart what is written in it, because the time is near.

REVELATION 1:3

For these commands are a lamp,
this teaching is a light,
and the corrections of discipline
are the way to life.

PROVERBS 6:23

When he was at the table with them, he took bread, gave thanks, broke it and began to give it to them. Then their eyes were opened and they recognized him, and he disappeared from their sight. They asked each other, "Were not our hearts burning within us while he talked with us on the road and opened the Scriptures to us?"

LUKE 24:30-32

REMBRANDT VAN RIJN

Being Met by God

I will betroth you in faithfulness,
and you will acknowledge the Lord.

HOSEA 2:20

Answer me quickly, O Lord; my spirit fails.
Do not hide your face from me
or I will be like those who go down to the pit.
Let the morning bring me word of your unfailing love,
for I have put my trust in you.
Show me the way I should go, for to you I lift up my soul.
Rescue me from my enemies, O Lord,
for I hide myself in you.
Teach me to do your will, for you are my God;
may your good Spirit lead me on level ground.

PSALM 143:7-10

But now in Christ Jesus you who once were far away
have been brought near through the blood of Christ.
For he himself is our peace, who has made the two one and
has destroyed the barrier, the dividing wall of hostility, by abolishing
in his flesh the law with its commandments and regulations.
His purpose was to create in himself one new man out of the two,
thus making peace, and in this one body to reconcile both of them
to God through the cross, by which he put to death their hostility.
He came and preached peace to you who were far away and peace
to those who were near. For through him we both have access
to the Father by one Spirit.

EPHESIANS 2:13-18

He will cover you with his feathers,
and under his wings you will find refuge;
his faithfulness will be your shield and rampart.

PSALM 91:4

Brotherhood

And Jonathan made a covenant with David because he loved him as himself. Jonathan took off the robe he was wearing and gave it to David, along with his tunic, and even his sword, his bow and his belt.

1 SAMUEL 18:3-4

I grieve for you, Jonathan my brother; you were very dear to me. Your love for me was wonderful, more wonderful than that of women.

2 SAMUEL 1:26

Whoever loves his brother lives in the light, and there is nothing in him to make him stumble. But whoever hates his brother is in the darkness and walks around in the darkness.

1 JOHN 2:10-11

A friend loves at all times, and a brother is born for adversity.

PROVERBS 17:17

GUSTAVE CAILLEBOTTE

Relationships

Accept one another, then, just as Christ accepted you, in order to bring praise to God.

ROMANS 15:7

A man of many companions may come to ruin, but there is a friend who sticks closer than a brother.

PROVERBS 18:24

Do nothing out of selfish ambition or vain conceit, but in humility consider others better than yourselves.

PHILIPPIANS 2:3

As iron sharpens iron,
so one man sharpens another.

PROVERBS 27:17

Bear with each other and forgive
whatever grievances you may have
against one another. Forgive as the Lord forgave you.

COLOSSIANS 3:13

Dear children, let us not love with
words or tongue but with actions and in truth.

1 JOHN 3:18

Seasons

Let there be lights in the expanse of the sky to separate the day from the night, and let them serve as signs to mark seasons and days and years, and let them be lights in the expanse of the sky to give light on the earth.

GENESIS 1:14-15

At the present time your plenty will supply what they need, so that in turn their plenty will supply what you need. Then there will be equality, as it is written: "He who gathered much did not have too much, and he who gathered little did not have too little."

2 CORINTHIANS 8:14-15

I am the Alpha and the Omega, says the Lord God, who is, and who was, and who is to come, the Almighty.

REVELATION 1:8

VINCENT VAN GOGH

Generations come and generations go,
but the earth remains for ever.
The sun rises and the sun sets,
and hurries back to where it rises.
The wind blows to the south and turns to the north;
round and round it goes, ever returning on its course.
All streams flow into the sea, yet the sea is never full.
To the place the streams come from, there they return again.
All things are wearisome,
more than one can say.
The eye never has enough of seeing,
nor the ear its fill of hearing.
What has been will be again,
what has been done will be done again;
there is nothing new under the sun.

ECCLESIASTES 1:4-9

Past

I will tell of the kindnesses of the Lord,
the deeds for which he is to be praised,
according to all the Lord has done for us—
yes, the many good things he has done for the house of Israel,
according to his compassion and many kindnesses.
He said, "Surely they are my people,
sons who will not be false to me"; and so he became their Savior.
In all their distress he too was distressed,
and the angel of his presence saved them.
In his love and mercy he redeemed them;
he lifted them up and carried them all the days of old.

ISAIAH 63:7-9

No one who puts his hand to the plough and looks back
is fit for service in the kingdom of God.

LUKE 9:62

Paul Cezanne

I pursued my enemies and overtook them;
I did not turn back till they were destroyed.
I crushed them so that they could not rise;
they fell beneath my feet.

PSALM 18:37-38

Brothers, I do not consider myself yet to have taken hold of it. But one thing I do: Forgetting what is behind and straining towards what is ahead, I press on towards the goal to win the prize for which God has called me heavenwards in Christ Jesus.

PHILIPPIANS 3:13-14

You turned my wailing into dancing;
you removed my sackcloth and clothed me with joy,
that my heart may sing to you and not be silent.
O Lord my God, I will give you thanks forever.

PSALM 30:11-12

Present

Therefore keep watch, because you do not know on what day your Lord will come. But understand this: If the owner of the house had known at what time of night the thief was coming, he would have kept watch and would not have let his house be broken into. So you also must be ready, because the Son of Man will come at an hour when you do not expect him.

MATTHEW 24:42-44

I tell you the truth, you will weep and mourn while the world rejoices. You will grieve, but your grief will turn to joy. A woman giving birth to a child has pain because her time has come; but when her baby is born she forgets the anguish because of her joy that a child is born into the world. So with you: Now is your time of grief, but I will see you again and you will rejoice, and no one will take away your joy.

JOHN 16:20-22

CLAUDE MONET

Do not say to your neighbor,
"Come back later; I'll give it tomorrow"—
when you now have it with you.

PROVERBS 3:28

But encourage one another daily,
as long as it is called Today, so that none of you
may be hardened by sin's deceitfulness.

HEBREWS 3:13

He who gathers crops in summer is a wise son,
but he who sleeps during harvest is a disgraceful son.

PROVERBS 10:5

Future

But the Counselor, the Holy Spirit, whom the Father will send in my name, will teach you all things and will remind you of everything I have said to you. Peace I leave with you; my peace I give you. I do not give to you as the world gives. Do not let your hearts be troubled and do not be afraid. You heard me say, "I am going away and I am coming back to you." If you loved me, you would be glad that I am going to the Father, for the Father is greater than I.

JOHN 14:26-28

My Presence will go with you, and I will give you rest.

EXODUS 33:14

I will betroth you to me for ever;
I will betroth you in righteousness and justice, in love and compassion.

HOSEA 2:19

For I know the plans I have for you,
declares the Lord, plans to prosper you and not to harm you,
plans to give you hope and a future.

JEREMIAH 29:11

All authority in heaven and on earth has been given to me.
Therefore go and make disciples of all nations, baptizing them in
the name of the Father and of the Son and of the Holy Spirit, and
teaching them to obey everything I have commanded you.
And surely I am with you always, to the very end of the age.

MATTHEW 28:18-20

Behold, I am coming soon! My reward is with me,
and I will give to everyone according to what he has done.
I am the Alpha and the Omega, the First and the Last,
the Beginning and the End.

REVELATION 22:12-13

CLAUDE MONET

Picture Credits:

Cover: William Henry Midwood, "Come to Daddy", 1867-71. Haynes Fine Art at the Bindery Galleries. Photo: The Bridgeman Art Library

Page 5: Otto Haslund, "A Concert: The Artist's Children and their Playmates", 1887. Statens Museum for Kunst, Copenhagen. Photo: Hans Petersen

Page 9: Constantin Hansen, "A Hunter shows a little Girl his Bag", 1832. Ny Carlsberg Glyptoteket, Copenhagen. Photo: Ny Carlsberg Glyptoteket

Page 12: Walter Leistikow, "Cloud Shadows", 1902. Staatliche Graphische Sammlung, München. Photo: AKG Berlin

Page 15: Maria Bashkirtseff, "The Meeting". Musée d'Orsay, Paris.

Page 19: Venician, "Father and Daughter", c. 1550. Kunsthistorisches Museum, Vienna. Photo: AKG Berlin / Erich Lessing

Page 21: Ilja Repin, "Portrait of Michail Iwanowitsch Glinka", 1887. Tretjakow-Galerie, Moskow. Photo: AKG Berlin

Page 24: Theo van Rysselberghe, "La lecture", 1903. Museum voor Schone Kunsten, Gent. Photo: AKG Berlin / Erich Lessing

Page 29: Vincent van Gogh, "The Sower", 1888. E. G. Buehrle Collection, Zürich. Photo: AKG Berlin

Page 32: Francois Gerard, "The Painter Jean-Baptiste Isabey and his Daughter Alexandrine," 1795. Musée du Louvre, Paris. Photo: AKG Berlin / Erich Lessing

Page 37: Paul Gauguin, "Road into the Mountains", 1891. The Toledo Museum of Art, Toledo. Photo: AKG Berlin / Erich Lessing

Page 40: Auguste Renoir, "The Lovers", 1875. Nationalgalerie, Prague. Photo: AKG Berlin / Erich Lessing

Page 43: Christen Dalsgaard, "Oh, won't He ever come?", 1879. The Hirschsprung Collection, Copenhagen. Photo: Hans Petersen

Page 47: Franz Bohumil Doubek, "O du fröhliche, o du selige, gnadenbringende Weihnachtszeit!", 1909. Photo: AKG Berlin

Page 49: Mary Cassatt, "Mother and Child", 1890s. Pushkin Museum, Moscow. Photo: The Bridgeman Art Library

Page 50: Otto Haslund, "A Concert: The Artist's Children and their Playmates", 1887. Statens Museum for Kunst, Copenhagen. Photo: Hans Petersen

Page 55: Peter Hansen, "Children skating outside Faaborg", 1901. Statens Museum for Kunst, Copenhagen. Photo: DOWIC Fotografi

Page 57: Peder Severin Krøyer, "The Forge", 1877. The Fine Art Society, London. Photo: The Bridgeman Art Library

Page 61: Ernst Josephson, "La joie de vivre", 1887. Statens Museum for Kunst, Copenhagen. Photo: Hans Petersen

Page 63: Caspar Wolf, "Thunderstorm and Lightning at the Lower Grindelwald Glacier", 1774/78. Aargauer Kunsthaus, Aarau. Photo: AKG Berlin
Page 67: Lovis Corinth, "Storm at Cap Ampeglio", 1912. Gemäldegalerie, Neue Meister, Dresden. Photo: AKG Berlin
Page 70: Albert Edelfelt, "Last Journey of a Child", 1879. Ateneumin Taidemuseo, Helsinki. Photo: AKG Berlin
Page 75: Frederic Bazille, "L'ambulance improvisee", 1865. Musée du Louvre, Paris. Photo: AKG Berlin / Erich Lessing
Page 79: Frants Henningsen, "A Funeral", 1883. Statens Museum for Kunst, Copenhagen. Photo: DOWIC Fotografi
Page 81: Gustav Klimt, "Birch forest", 1903. Galerie im Belvedere, Vienna. Photo: AKG Berlin / Erich Lessing
Page 83: Vincent van Gogh, "The Siesta", 1889/90. Musée d'Orsay, Paris. Photo: AKG Berlin / Erich Lessing
Page 86: Vilhelm Hammershøi, "Young Beech Trees. Arresødal", 1904. The Hirschsprung Collection, Copenhagen. Photo: AKG Berlin
Page 89: Christian Krogh, "In the Tub", 1889. Statens Museum for Kunst, Copenhagen. Photo: Hans Petersen
Page 92: Camille Pissarro, "Paysage a Eragny; eglise et ferme d'Eragny", 1895. Musée d'Orsay, Paris. Photo: AKG Berlin / Erich Lessing
Page 97: Jean Francois Millet, "Angelus", 1858/59. Musée d'Orsay, Paris. Photo: AKG Berlin / Erich Lessing
Page 100: Hugo Simberg, "Spring Evening with melting Snow", 1897. Ateneumin Taidemuseo, Helsinki. Photo: AKG Berlin
Page 105: Halfdan Egedius, "From Vaga", 1894. Rasmus Meyers Samlinger, Bergen. Photo: AKG Berlin
Page 109: Rembrandt van Rijn, "Supper at Emmaus", 1648. Statens Museum for Kunst, Copenhagen. Photo: DOWIC Fotografi
Page 113: Gustave Caillebotte, "Planing the Floorboards", 1875. Musée d'Orsay, Paris. Photo: The Bridgeman Art Library
Page 117: Vincent van Gogh, "Starry Night over the Rhone", 1888. Musée d'Orsay, Paris. Photo: AKG Berlin / Erich Lessing
Page 120: Paul Cezanne, "Blue Landscape", 1904/06. I. A. Morosov Collection. Photo: AKG Berlin
Page 123: Claude Monet, "Hauling in of a Boat, Honfleur", 1864. Memorial Art Gallery of the University of Rochester, New York. Photo: AKG Berlin
Page 127: Claude Monet, "Waterlily Pond," 1899. National Gallery, London. Photo: The Bridgeman Art Library